THE

2012 - 2013

ALABAMA

CRIMSON

TIDE:

SEC CHAMPIONS, THE PURSUIT OF
BACK-TO-BACK BCS NATIONAL
CHAMPIONSHIPS,
& A COLLEGE FOOTBALL LEGACY

Dan Fathow

MEGALODON ENTERTAINMENT, LLC.

Published by Megalodon Entertainment, LLC. (USA)
www.MegalodonEntertainment.com

First Printing: January 2013

Copyright © 2013 Megalodon Entertainment LLC. All rights reserved.

All rights reserved under the International and Pan-American Copyright conventions. No part of this publication may be reproduced, or transmitted by any means in any form (electronic, photocopying, mechanical, recording, or any other method), without the specific written permission of the publisher. Please, direct questions to info@megalodonentertainment.com.

Printed in the United States of America.

ISBN: 978-1-61589-038-5
ISBN-10: 1-61589-038-6

The BCS, Alabama Crimson Tide, NFL, college football, and all team names are ™ of their respective owners. No affiliation to any teams, players, or intellectual properties is claimed or implied by this publication.

BULK INQUERIES:
Quantity discounts are available on bulk orders of this novel for educational, fund-raising, promotional, and special sales purposes.
For details, please contact www.MegalodonEntertainment.com

2012 Alabama Crimson Tide 3

CHECK OUT ANOTHER GREAT BOOK FROM MEGALODON ENTERTAINMENT LLC

FROM LEWIS ALEMAN, BESTSELLING AUTHOR OF COLD STREAK & FACES IN TIME

Simon is a vampire, prowling through the dark New Orleans streets that pulse with wild adventure and fangs gleaming in the shadows. He's spent the last few decades as a recluse, aching over a lost love. Now, he's put it behind him, thirsting to fulfill the raging inner need he's deprived himself for so long.

Ruby feels isolated and out of place--lonely, shy, but too strong-minded to go along with the crowd. All that changes when she is dragged out for her birthday and ends up dancing with Simon-- mysterious, blue-eyed, and gorgeous. Her body tingles watching his muscled form move--so fast, so smooth, so powerful. His smile is otherworldly, and his kiss charges her with electric energy. All seems to be going well until three other vampires appear in the crowd, turning the dance floor into a horror show.

THE ANTI-VAMPIRE TALE

Bestselling Author of FACES IN TIME and COLD STREAK

LEWIS ALEMAN

REAL VAMPIRES...DON'T SPARKLE

WWW.LEWISALEMAN.COM
FACEBOOK.COM/LEWISALEMAN
YOUTUBE.COM/LEWISALEMAN

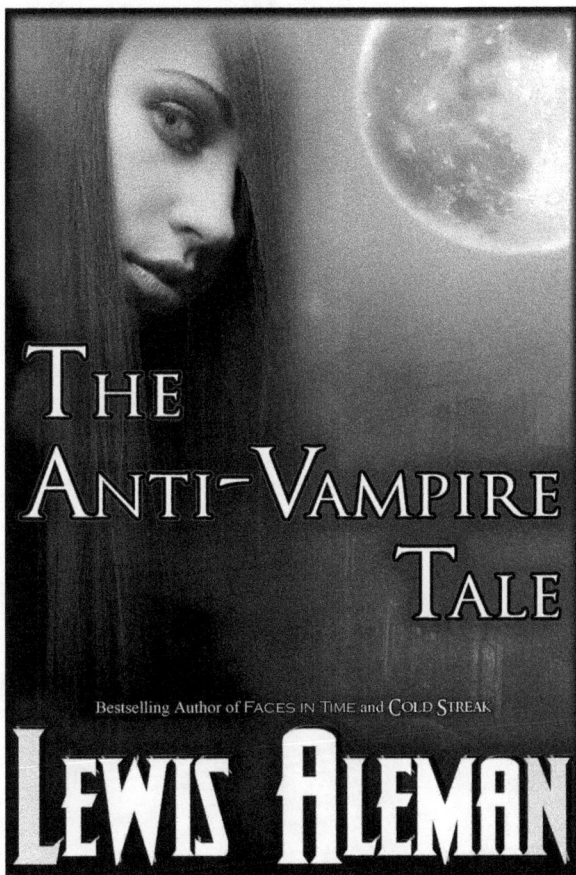

THE
2012
ALABAMA
CRIMSON
TIDE:

SEC CHAMPIONS & A COLLEGE FOOTBALL LEGACY

Dan Fathow

MEGALODON ENTERTAINMENT, LLC.

TABLE OF CONTENTS

PART I: 2012 THE MAGNIFICENT SEASON

PART II: THE BCS NATIONAL CHAMPIONSHIP THE MATCHUP VS. NOTRE DAME.

PART III: THE SABAN FACTOR

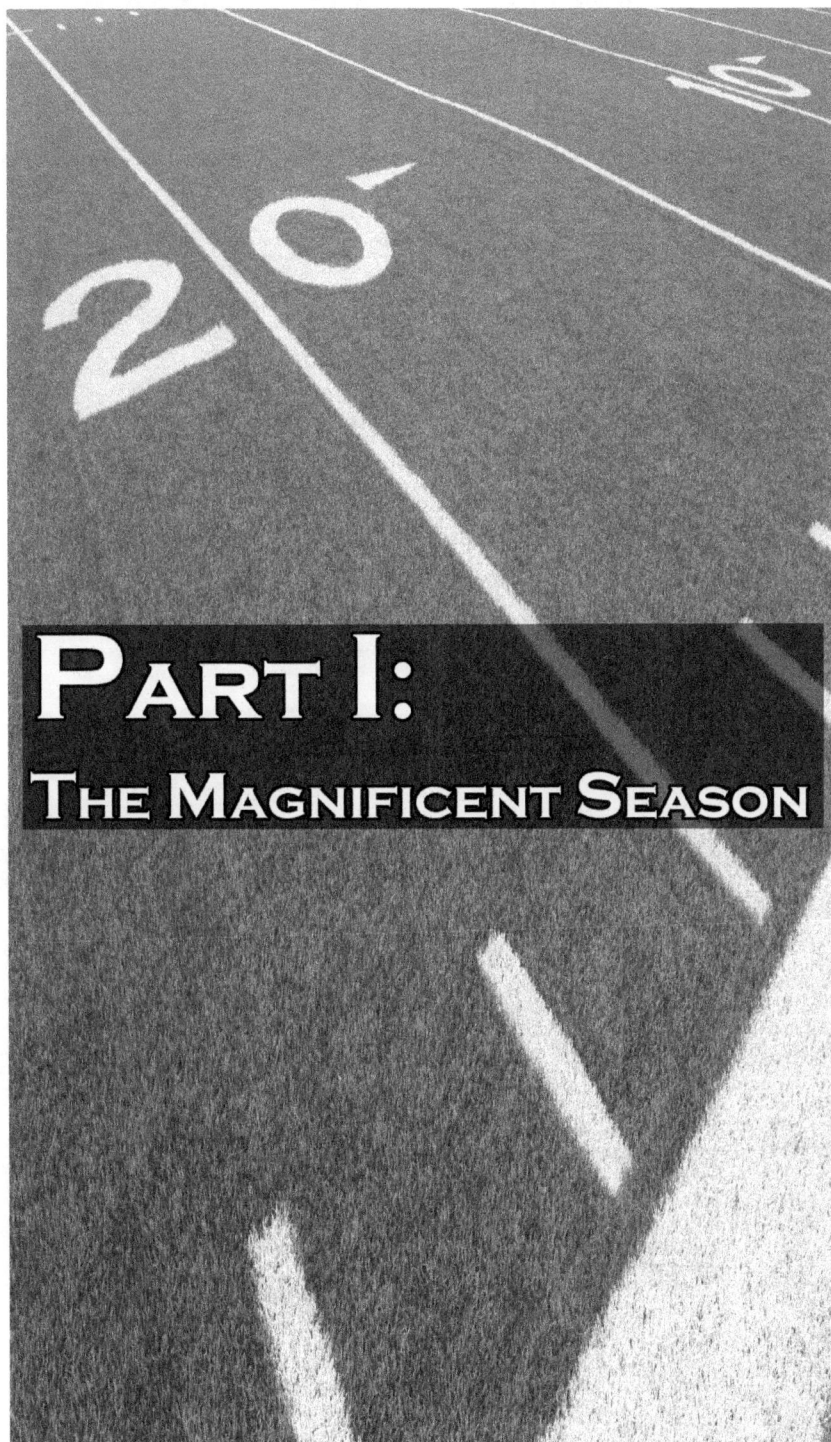

PART I:
THE MAGNIFICENT SEASON

GAME 1

September 1, 2012
Cowboys Stadium – Arlington, TX

Teams	1st	2nd	3rd	4th	Total
#8Michigan	0	7	7	0	14
#2 Alabama	21	10	3	7	41

GAME SUMMARY

The opening game of the season saw the defending national champions, the Alabama Crimson Tide, ranked as the #2 team in all of college football, which raised the ire of most fans. Many components of the previous year's team were still in place, including senior quarterback A.J. McCarron, revered head coach Nick Saban, and the team's trademark strong defense. Many fans thought: *with all of these elements in place, shouldn't the defending champs be ranked #1?*

Whatever the reason for the #2 ranking, perhaps all that it accomplished was to light a fire underneath the Crimson Tide to prove to the world that they were indeed still the best in college football. It would seem that this may have been the case as Alabama routed the #8 Michigan Wolverines, 41-14. Alabama was certainly picked to win, but not by a staggering 27 points.

A.J. McCarron was only 1 yard shy of throwing for 200 yards. He also connected for 2 passing touchdowns with 0 interceptions. The 0 interceptions was a stat that he would repeat game after game, which was a crucial element in the team's season-long success.

T.J. Yeldon had a banner day rushing for 111 yards and 1 touchdown. Eddie Lacy also rushed for a touchdown.

On the receiving end, DeAndrew White and Michael Williams both caught touchdown passes from McCarron.

The Crimson Tide kickers had a great game too. Jeremy Shelley was perfect, accounting for 8 of the team's points, going 1/1 on field goals and hitting all 5 extra points. Cade Foster may have only gone 1 for 2 on field goals, but the one that he did sling through the uprights was from an impressive 51 yards away.

The Crimson Tide won the turnover war 3-1, only giving up 1 lost fumble to the Wolverines. On the other side of the ball, Alabama nabbed 3 interceptions from Michigan, which had a huge impact on this game, 1 of which was run all the way back for a touchdown by C.J. Mosley.

The Alabama defense held the Wolverines to only 69 rushing yards, while their own team racked up 232 running yards. This huge disparity in the ground games was what put the Crimson Tide way ahead in total yards, 431 Alabama yards to 269 Michigan yards.

It was an impressive performance out of the gate on all aspects of the ball, showcasing the well-rounded strengths of the 2012 Crimson Tide team, and it was a sign of great things to come.

TEAM LEADERS

Passing

A.J. McCarron #12
199 Yards, 2 Touchdowns, 0 Interceptions
(11/21, 52 Comp %)

Rushing

T.J. Yeldon #4
111 Yards on 11 Carries
10.09 Yards per Carry
1 Touchdown

Jalston Fowler #45
67 Yards on 8 Carries
8.38 Yards per Carry
0 Touchdowns

Eddie Lacy #42
35 Yards on 9 Carries
3.89 Yards per Carry
1 Touchdown

Receiving

Kevin Norwood #83
53 Yards on 3 Receptions
17.66 Yards per Reception
0 Touchdowns

DeAndrew White #7
51 Yards on 1 Reception
51 Yards per Reception
1 Touchdown Reception

Michael Williams #89
2 Yards on 1 Reception
2 Yards per Reception
1 Touchdown Reception

Kicking

Jeremy Shelley #5
8 Points Total
1/1 Field Goals (22 Yards)
5/5 Extra Points

Cade Foster #43
3 Points Total
1/2 Field Goals (51 Yards)
0/0 Extra Points

Interceptions

Dee Milliner #28
1 Interception

C.J. Mosley #32
1 Interception (Ran back for a touchdown)

Dillon Lee #25
1 Interception

THE BOTTOM LINE

1 - 0

GAME 2

September 8, 2012
Bryant-Denny Stadium - Tuscaloosa, AL

Teams	1st	2nd	3rd	4th	Total
WKU	0	0	0	0	**0**
#1 Alabama	14	7	7	7	**35**

GAME SUMMARY

After a dominating victory over #8 Michigan the week before, the Alabama Crimson Tide faced a 1-0 but unranked West Kentucky University team at home in Tuscaloosa. Alabama was the heavily-picked favorite in this encounter, but a 35-0 shutout was a very impressive performance.

After their previous victory, Alabama came into this game as the #1-ranked team in the country. Their performance certainly supported their newly-gained ranking.

This was a stellar game for quarterback A.J. McCarron, as he threw for 219 yards and 4 touchdowns on 14 of 19 passes, earning a 73.6 completion percentage.

While Alabama threw for 47 more yards than their opponent, they also rushed for 57 more yards, had 23 less penalty yards, and had 0 turnovers to their opponents' staggering 4 turnovers (3 fumbles and 1 interception). That wins ballgames. Couple that with superior passing, and it equals complete domination.

TEAM LEADERS

Passing

A.J. McCarron #10
219 Yards, 4 Touchdowns, 0 Interceptions
(14/19, 73.6 Comp %)

Rushing

Eddie Lacy #42
36 Yards on 9 Carries
4.0 Yards per Carry
0 Touchdowns

Kenyan Drake #17
32 Yards on 1 Carries
32 Yards per Carry
1 Touchdown

T.J. Yeldon #4
25 Yards on 6 Carries
4.16 Yards per Carry
2 Touchdowns

Receiving

Kevin Norwood #83
92 Yards on 3 Receptions
30.66 Yards per Reception
2 Touchdowns

T.J. Yeldon #4
47 Yards on 4 Receptions
11.75 Yards per Reception
0 Touchdowns

Christion Jones #22
47 Yards on 3 Receptions
15.66 Yards per Reception
2 Touchdowns

Kicking

Jeremy Shelley #5
5 Points Total
0/0 Field Goals
5/5 Extra Points

Interceptions

Deion Belue #13
1 Interception

DAN FATHOW 18

THE BOTTOM LINE

2 - 0

GAME 3

September 15, 2012
Razorback Stadium - Fayetteville, AR

Teams	1st	2nd	3rd	4th	Total
Arkansas	0	0	0	0	**0**
#1 Alabama	7	17	14	14	**52**

GAME SUMMARY

Week 3 proved to be more of the same of week 2: another unranked team and another complete trouncing, ending in a shutout.

The Arkansas Razorbacks were simply no match for the domination machine of the Alabama Crimson Tide. Some major highlights of the game were Eddie Lacy's 3 rushing touchdowns.

2 shutouts in 2 weeks are impressive regardless of who the opponents may be. A shutout is darn near a one-sided, perfect game. The combined score from weeks 2 and 3 has Alabama at 87 points and opponents at 0. That is exactly what a #1-ranked team is supposed to do when it faces 2 unranked teams. The Crimson Tide were proving they deserved their top spot, even if their opponents were not up to the same level of competition as they were.

The game was so well at hand that freshman backup quarterback Phillip Ely got some game play, connecting on 2 of 3 passes for 15 yards.

With 6 rushing touchdowns and 213 rushing yards, the Crimson Tide ground game was really firing.

Once again, Alabama won the turnover war 2-0 over the Razorbacks.

TEAM LEADERS

Passing

A.J. McCarron #10
189 Yards, 1 Touchdown, 0 Interceptions
(11/16, 68.7 Comp %)

Phillip Ely #12
15 Yards, 0 Touchdowns, 0 Interceptions
(2/3, 66.67 Comp %)

Rushing

Kenyan Drake #17
57 Yards on 6 Carries
9.5 Yards per Carry
1 Touchdown

Eddie Lacy #42
55 Yards on 12 Carries
4.58 Yards per Carry
3 Touchdowns

T.J. Yeldon #4
55 Yards on 13 Carries
4.23 Yards per Carry
1 Touchdown

Blake Sims #6
25 Yards on 2 Carries
12.5 Yards per Carry
1 Touchdown

Receiving

Christion Jones #22
74 Yards on 3 Receptions
24.66 Yards per Reception
0 Touchdowns

Amari Cooper #9
46 Yards on 2 Receptions
23 Yards per Reception
1 Touchdown

Michael Williams #89
20 Yards on 2 Receptions
10 Yards per Reception
0 Touchdowns

Kicking

Jeremy Shelley #5
7 Points Total
0/0 Field Goals
7/7 Extra Points

Cade Foster #43
3 Points Total
1/2 Field Goals
0/0 Extra Points

Interceptions

Ha'Sean Clinton-Dix #6
1 Interception

Vinnie Sunseri #3
1 Interception

THE BOTTOM LINE

3 - 0

GAME 4

September 22, 2012
Bryant-Denny Stadium - Tuscaloosa, AL

Teams	1st	2nd	3rd	4th	Total
Florida Atlantic	0	0	0	7	7
#1 Alabama	14	16	3	7	**40**

GAME SUMMARY

Game 4 marked the 3rd game in a row that the Alabama Crimson Tide had beaten its opponent by at least 33 points. In fact, if not for a lone 4th-quarter touchdown by Florida Atlantic, it would have been the 3rd shutout in a row from the hands of the Crimson Tide defense. Before that score, Alabama had scored 134 points, and its opponents had scored 0 over the course of the last two games and most of this game.

A.J. McCarron had a great day with 3 touchdown passes and no interceptions. The big play of the game was an 85-yard pass to wide receiver Kenny Bell for a touchdown. This was also the second game in which McCarron threw for over 200 yards this season.

Eddie Lacy rushed for over 100 yards, and Kenyan Drake ran in a touchdown. With 1 rushing touchdown and 3 passing touchdowns, the Crimson Tide were scoring both in the air and on the ground.

The kicking game was also flawless accounting for 10 points. Jeremy Shelley and Cade Foster combined to hit 4/4 field goals (2 each), and Shelley hit all 4 extra points. Foster hit the longest field goal of the day with a stout 52-yarder.

The only area of the game that Alabama did not win was the turnover war. Florida did not give up any turnovers, while Alabama had 1 lone fumble. As the lopsided score shows, this 1 fumble did not harm the Crimson Tide very much at all.

TEAM LEADERS

Passing

A.J. McCarron #10
212 Yards, 3 Touchdowns, 0 Interceptions
(15/25, 60 Comp %)

Rushing

Eddie Lacy #42
106 Yards on 15 Carries
7.06 Yards per Carry
0 Touchdowns

T.J. Yeldon #4
63 Yards on 10 Carries
6.3 Yards per Carry
0 Touchdowns

Kenyan Drake #17
35 Yards on 5 Carries
7 Yards per Carry
1 Touchdown

Receiving

Kenny Bell #7
85 Yards on 1 Reception
85 Yards per Reception
1 Touchdown

Amari Cooper #9
65 Yards on 4 Receptions
16.25 Yards per Reception
0 Touchdowns

Christion Jones #22
35 Yards on 1 Reception
35 Yards per Reception
0 Touchdowns

Michael Williams #89
25 Yards on 4 Receptions
6.25 Yards per Reception
0 Touchdowns

DeAndrew White #2
17 Yards on 4 Receptions
4.25 Yards per Reception
1 Touchdown

Kicking

Jeremy Shelley #5
10 Points Total
2/2 Field Goals
4/4 Extra Points

Cade Foster #43
6 Points Total
2/2 Field Goals
0/0 Extra Points

Interceptions

None

THE BOTTOM LINE

4 - 0

GAME 5

September 29, 2012
Bryant-Denny Stadium – Tuscaloosa, AL

Teams	1st	2nd	3rd	4th	Total
Ole Miss	0	7	7	0	14
#1 Alabama	6	21	0	6	33

GAME SUMMARY

The most unusual occurrence in the game was that for the first time this season Alabama actually trailed an opponent in points. So, the Ole Miss Rebels only had a 1-point lead for a miniscule 8 seconds of the game, but it was interesting to see how the Crimson Tide would respond to being down in points for the first time. The Alabama team responded with force, eventually beating Ole Miss by 19 points.

Ole Miss came into the game at 3-1, appearing to be a much stronger team than what their final season record of 6-6 (3-5 in the SEC) would later indicate. The 2012 Alabama Crimson Tide were a great litmus test for any aspiring team, exposing all of their weaknesses and pushing them to their limits on both offense and defense. The Tide certainly pointed out some of Ole Miss's shortcomings.

Alabama had a total 305 offensive yards, and they won the turnover battle 3-1. McCarron had a good day with 180 yards, 2 touchdowns, and 0 interceptions. The time of possession tells the story of this game. The Tide had the ball for

9:58 longer than Ole Miss, and that was a lot of time for this team to inflict some serious scoreboard damage.

Ole Miss put up the best contest against the Crimson Tide thus far in the season, losing by 19 points, which was the smallest margin of defeat for any Alabama opponent to date. In retrospect, it was a valiant fight put up against a stronger team that would become SEC champions on their way to the BCS National Championship Game.

One very impressive standout statistic is that after 5 games, Alabama quarterback A.J. McCarron has thrown for 12 touchdowns with *0* interceptions.

Wide receiver Amari Cooper had a great day, catching 8 passes for 84 yards and 2 touchdowns.

On a side note, this marks the first game in which Alabama did not score a rushing touchdown, although the team did still rush for 125 yards.

Alabama's kicking played a huge part in this game, accounting for 15 total points. From the foot of Jeremy Shelley, 45.45% of the Crimson Tide's points were scored on 4 field goals and 3 extra points, which was achieved flawlessly without missing a single attempt through the uprights.

TEAM LEADERS

Passing

A.J. McCarron #10
180 Yards, 2 Touchdowns, 0 Interceptions
(22/30, 73.33 Comp %)

Rushing

Eddie Lacy #42
82 Yards on 19 Carries
4.32 Yards per Carry
0 Touchdowns

T.J. Yeldon #4
38 Yards on 10 Carries
3.8 Yards per Carry
0 Touchdowns

Receiving

Amari Cooper #9
84 Yards on 8 Receptions
10.5 Yards per Reception
2 Touchdowns

Kevin Norwood #83
20 Yards on 2 Receptions
10 Yards per Reception
0 Touchdowns

Christion Jones #22
19 Yards on 2 Receptions
9.5 Yards per Reception
0 Touchdowns

Kicking

Jeremy Shelley #5

DAN FATHOW 30

15 Points Total
4/4 Field Goals
3/3 Extra Points

Interceptions

Robert Lester #37
1 Interception

Lee Milliner #28
1 Interception

Deion Belue #13
1 Interception

THE BOTTOM LINE

5 - 0

GAME 6

October 13, 2012
Faurot Field – Columbia, MO

Teams	1st	2nd	3rd	4th	Total
Missouri	0	7	3	0	11
#1 Alabama	21	7	0	14	41

GAME SUMMARY

Week 6 was a return to total domination for the Alabama Crimson Tide, beating their opponent by 32 points. Coming into this game Missouri was unranked with a 3-3 record. Not many picked Missouri to have a good chance at winning, but not many were picking this game to be a 32-point trouncing either.

These 30+ point victories provided a counter-attack to those critics who were saying that Alabama was undoubtedly a good team, but that they had only played 1 ranked team 6 games into the season. Few doubted Alabama's greatness, but many pointed out that they had barely been tested against other great teams. In all fairness, the best team Alabama had played at this point was a #8 Michigan, who by season's end would end up ranked #18 with a record of only 8-5. However, it must be pointed out that an untested team can still be the best team in all of college football. Just because they have not been put to the ultimate test does not mean that they would not pass it. This may have provided some motivation for the Alabama team to prove they deserved their number 1 ranking by not just beating their inferior competition but demolishing them. Beating a team by 32 points on the road in their opponent's home stadium makes a powerful statement.

Alabama's offense put up a total of 533 total yards, while the Crimson Tide defense held Missouri to just 129 yards. That's clear mastery on both sides of the ball.

This game marked the return of multiple rushing touchdowns by the Crimson Tide, amassing an awesome total of 6 touchdowns, 5 of those being split between Eddie Lacy and T.J. Yeldon. Lacy and Yeldon combined for a total of 321 yards, meaning they basically drove the ball down the field from one end zone to the other 3.21 times all by themselves.

However, it also marked the first game in which A.J. McCarron did not throw a passing touchdown. It should be pointed out that after 6 games McCarron still had not thrown a single interception.

Alabama put up explosive 1st and 4th quarters, combining for 35 of their 42 points. In the second quarter, the Crimson Tide only matched the touchdown put up by Missouri, and surprisingly Missouri outscored Alabama in the 3rd quarter with a field goal.

Other notables during this game were a half-an-hour-plus lightning delay, poor weather conditions throughout, and a Missouri team that had its starting quarterback out with an injury.

TEAM LEADERS

Passing

A.J. McCarron #10
171 Yards, 0 Touchdowns, 0 Interceptions
(16/21, 76.19 Comp %)

Rushing

Eddie Lacy #42
177 Yards on 18 Carries
9.83 Yards per Carry
3 Touchdowns

T.J. Yeldon #4
144 Yards on 18 Carries
8 Yards per Carry
2 Touchdowns

Kenyan Drake #17
11 Yards on 4 Carries
2.75 Yards per Carry
1 Touchdown

Receiving

Kenny Bell #7
46 Yards on 2 Receptions
23 Yards per Reception
0 Touchdowns

Amari Cooper #9
41 Yards on 4 Receptions
10.25 Yards per Reception
0 Touchdowns

Kevin Norwood #83
25 Yards on 3 Receptions
8.33 Yards per Reception
0 Touchdowns

Christion Jones #22
19 Yards on 2 Receptions
9.5 Yards per Reception
0 Touchdowns

Kicking

Jeremy Shelley #5
6 Points Total
0/0 Field Goals
6/6 Extra Points

Interceptions

Ha'Sean Clinton-Dix #6
1 Interception

Vinnie Sunseri #3
1 Interception

THE BOTTOM LINE

6 - 0

GAME 7

October 20, 2012
Neyland Stadium – Knoxville, TN

Teams	1st	2nd	3rd	4th	Total
Tennessee	3	7	0	3	**13**
#1 Alabama	7	16	7	14	**44**

GAME SUMMARY

The seventh week of the 2012 season was another blowout provided courtesy of the Alabama Crimson Tide, beating the Tennessee Volunteers by 31 points, making 30-point victories seem commonplace for the Tide.

Coming into the game, Alabama was undefeated at 6-0 and Tennessee was 3-3 (0-3 in the SEC), so the lopsided score is about what one would expect in this matchup.

In this one-sided affair, Alabama racked up 306 yards in total offense to 203 by Tennessee. The Crimson Tide also won the turnover war 2-1, and held ball possession for 13:34 longer than the Volunteers.

The most notable performance came from quarterback A.J. McCarron, who burned up 306 yards passing on a 77.22 completion percentage for 4 touchdowns and 0 interceptions. Those numbers match some of the top-rated quarterbacks in the NFL on a good day. Granted that pro QB's are not facing off against the 2012 Tennessee Volunteers, it was still a very impressive performance. And for those of you keeping score, it was then 7 games down with 0 interceptions for McCarron.

The kicking game, which had been solid all year, was a mixed bag in this contest. Jeremy Shelley was perfect, going 1/1 on field goals (from 34 yards) and 5/5 on extra points. Cade Foster, who had proven to be a consistent long field goal threat, went 0/2 on field goals in this game.

By this point in the season, critics were screaming that all Alabama had done was beat a very over-ranked Michigan team and a bunch of unranked opponents. Fortunately for all involved, Alabama had dominated all of their opponents thus far, albeit lesser teams, and would face 4 ranked teams, 2 in the top 5, before the season would be over. All questions would be answered, and all doubt would be assuaged.

TEAM LEADERS

Passing

A.J. McCarron #10
306 Yards, 4 Touchdowns, 0 Interceptions
(17/22, 77.22 Comp %)

Rushing

T.J. Yeldon #4
129 Yards on 15 Carries
8.6 Yards per Carry
2 Touchdowns

Eddie Lacy #42
79 Yards on 17 Carries
4.65 Yards per Carry
0 Touchdowns

Kenyan Drake #17
22 Yards on 4 Carries
5.5 Yards per Carry
0 Touchdowns

Receiving

Amari Cooper #9
162 Yards on 7 Receptions
23.14 Yards per Reception
2 Touchdowns

Kenny Bell #7
68 Yards on 2 Receptions
34 Yards per Reception
1 Touchdown

Kevin Norwood #83
43 Yards on 2 Receptions
21.5 Yards per Reception
0 Touchdowns

Michael Williams #89
6 Yards on 2 Receptions
3 Yards per Reception
1 Touchdown

Kicking

Jeremy Shelley #5
8 Points Total
1/1 Field Goals
5/5 Extra Points

Cade Foster #43
0 Points Total
0/2 Field Goals
0/0 Extra Points

Interceptions

Robert Lester #37
1 Interception

C.J. Mosley #32
1 Interception

THE BOTTOM LINE

7 - 0

GAME 8

October 27, 2012
Bryant-Denny Stadium – Tuscaloosa, AL

Teams	1st	2nd	3rd	4th	Total
#11 Mississippi State	0	0	0	7	7
#1 Alabama	14	10	0	14	**38**

GAME SUMMARY

Finally, the Alabama Crimson Tide were given the opportunity to battle another ranked team in that of #11 Mississippi State. What Alabama needed to silence critics that felt the team hadn't yet proven itself against real competition was a decisive victory against the Bulldogs. What Alabama provided was a near-shutout in a 31-point victory over a #11-ranked team. Not only did they win, but they dismantled the Mississippi State Bulldogs as easily as they had any of their other opponents.

Quarterback A.J. McCarron had a great day as he threw for over 200 yards with 2 touchdowns. And, yes, after 8 games, McCarron still had not thrown a single interception. In addition, Freshman quarterback Phillip Ely got into the game and threw a 27-yard touchdown pass to Eddie Lacy.

While the defense allowed 209 yards passing, which is nearly as much as Alabama's offense was able to earn at 235 passing yards, the defense shut down the Bulldogs' running game, holding them to only 47 yards while their own team rushed for 179 yards. The defense also capitalized on key plays, forcing 3 turnovers (2 fumbles and 1 interception). The turnovers and difference in running games were where this game was really won.

TEAM LEADERS

Passing

A.J. McCarron #10
208 Yards, 2 Touchdowns, 0 Interceptions
(16/23, 69.56 Comp %)

Phillip Ely #12
27 Yards, 1 Touchdown, 0 Interceptions
(1/1, 100 Comp %)

Rushing

T.J. Yeldon #4
84 Yards on 10 Carries
8.4 Yards per Carry
1 Touchdown

Kenyan Drake #17
47 Yards on 8 Carries
5.88 Yards per Carry
1 Touchdown

Eddie Lacy #42
26 Yards on 10 Carries
2.6 Yards per Carry
0 Touchdowns

Receiving

Kenny Bell #7
57 Yards on 1 Receptions
57 Yards per Reception
1 Touchdown

Eddie Lacy #42
51 Yards on 4 Receptions
12.75 Yards per Carry
1 Touchdown

Amari Cooper #9
47 Yards on 4 Receptions
11.75 Yards per Reception
0 Touchdowns

Michael Williams #89
38 Yards on 5 Receptions
7.6 Yards per Reception
1 Touchdown

Kicking

Jeremy Shelley #5
8 Points Total
1/1 Field Goals
5/5 Extra Points

Interceptions

Robert Lester #37
1 Interception

THE BOTTOM LINE

8 - 0

GAME 9

November 3, 2012
Tiger Stadium – Baton Rouge, LA

Teams	1st	2nd	3rd	4th	Total
#5 LSU	3	0	7	7	21
#1 Alabama	0	3	0	3	17

GAME SUMMARY

The Rivalry

The rivalry between the University of Alabama Crimson Tide and the Louisiana State University Tigers is one of the, if not *the* most, widely known and most competitive rivalries in all of college football.

The last two times these teams met were in a game dubbed *The Game of the Century* and the 2012 BCS Championship Game. What is interesting about these two games is that the first game was a defensive battle that only resulted in 15 points, combined from both teams, and the second meeting was the BCS National Championship Game, which due to an unexpected and particularly poor performance from LSU, was the third-lowest rated BCS Championship Game ever. That's a far cry from the game of the century (which is what these teams meeting earlier in the season was expected to be), but most of the blame can certainly be placed on LSU's poor performance, especially that of ineffective quarterback Jordan Jefferson, who was truly not able to muster anything all game against Alabama's defense.

Why was The Game of the Century a bust?

The Game of the Century was the title generated by the sports media for the contest involving the undefeated, #1-ranked LSU Tigers and the undefeated, #2-ranked Alabama Crimson Tide on Saturday November 5, 2011 at 7:00 p.m.

Adding to the media frenzy was that not only were #1 and #2 meeting, guaranteeing an end to someone's perfect season, but LSU was facing off against its longtime rival whose head coach is none other than The Tiger's former head honcho, Nick Saban. Everything about the game had high-profile, smash-mouth, grudge-match football written all over it.

As usual, the media's practice of hyping something up to epicly ridiculous proportions left many viewers feeling disappointed when they finally watched the game. The game was a defensive contest, which was certainly out of style in 2011, a time when 3 different NFL quarterbacks were poised to shatter the all-time season passing record (which was indeed accomplished by Drew Brees about 8 weeks later). With that kind of an exciting, high-scoring football atmosphere, it was indeed hard to appreciate a 9-6 defensive war as "the game of the century," especially when Alabama's poor kicking had more to do with their loss than the Tiger's offense.

Being that these 2 teams would soon have their rematch in the national championship, there was definitely validity to some of the hype. In the media's defense, LSU and Alabama were certainly the 2 best teams in college football (their end of year records proved that) at the time, and it should have been the game of the year, if not the game of the decade. The game of the century is another story.

Fast Forward to 2012...

The November 3, 2012 contest between #1 Alabama and #5 LSU in many ways was a superior game than its over-hyped Game of the Century from the previous season.

1. A final score of 21-17 is a much more exciting game for contemporary college football fans than the 9-6 defensive battle of the previous year. Despite both contests coming down to the wire, more points equals more excitement. Maybe it's a result of shortening attention spans inhibiting modern audiences from appreciating a low-scoring defense affair, but regardless of the reason, high-scoring games are currently much more popular than lower scoring ones, despite how amazing the defense may be playing. It may be a sad indictment of society, but it's reality.

2. Pre-Game Drama:

#1 vs #2 is an artificial matchup. What does that mean? #1 and #2 teams are picked via the flawed BCS system that no one except the BCS seems to have any faith in whatsoever as being a fair method of picking college football's best teams. It's artificial for #1 and #2 to hate each other as if they're natural-born, mortal enemies. Having gone all season undefeated and then facing another undefeated team for bragging rights as the greatest team in the land is a much stronger motivation to win and fight than a mid-season battle of #1 and #2. It's actually amazing that the teams that were #1 and #2 after game 8 or 9 were still #1 and #2 at the season's end. Try betting on that both the #1 and #2 ranked teams at 8 games into the season will be in the Championship Game, and see how it turns out. (Going into the 8th game in the 2012 season, Notre Dame was ranked 5th, and after the game, they were still only ranked 3rd. Being that they ended up as #1, ranking at the 8th game of the season is not the be-all end-all the media makes it out to be).

In some ways, the 2012 matchup of #1 Alabama and #5 LSU had a lot more heat between the teams. Heat equals motivation, much more so than a media circus, which often does little more than distract athletes resulting in poor play. Before Alabama belittled LSU in the 2012 BCS Championship Game, LSU was being compared to the greatest college football teams of all-time. There was even discussion that if LSU lost to Alabama, they would have still already earned at least half of the national title by having an undefeated season and having already beaten the Crimson Tide earlier that year. However, Alabama slaughtered LSU so badly that no one could even try to argue with a straight face that LSU deserved half of the national championship. That kind of embarrassment is a strong motivation to play harder, especially after rising so high to instantly fall so low. Being compared to the greatest of all time to being the joke of the sports world is a hard slap in the face, and it can certainly be a motivator for a determined athlete for vindication.

Also, motivating LSU was their stunning loss to #10 Florida on October 6th. If the Tigers were to have any hopes at all of making it to the big game again, they had to beat the Crimson Tide (along with all of their other opponents) or it was all over for them. It truly was a win or be eliminated situation for the Tigers, which is a survival motivator. By comparison, in the previous year's matchup, either team could have lost and still made it to the National Championship (as did the Crimson Tide). This game was much more of a do-or-die situation for the Tigers than the dubious Game of the Century.

On Alabama's side, they also had strong motivation. The criticism that was eating at Alabama all year was that they hadn't beaten any good teams. They beat #8 Michigan in week 1, a team that was sorely overrated, and they had a great win in the previous week against #11 Mississippi State. But, that was only 2 victories against ranked teams. LSU would provide the Tide's first matchup against a top-

5 team all year. Throw on top of that the national rivalry and that LSU was the only team to beat Alabama in the 2012 season, and you get some powerful motivation to win this game. This was a game of respect for Alabama. As an 8-0 team with many impressive 30+ point victories, it must have been hard to hear critics say that the Crimson Tide were untested. This was to be their test, and the nation was watching.

How It All Went Down...

LSU did indeed provide Alabama's strongest threat thus far in the season. The game was hard-fought and a monumental test for both teams. Basically, it was college football at its best.

LSU had more total yards than Alabama, 435 to 331. LSU also won the turnover battle, 2-0. Furthermore, Alabama was only 1-9 on 3rd down efficiency, where LSU was 10-20. Perhaps the most damning evidence was that LSU had possession of the ball for nearly twice the time that Alabama did, 39:15 to 20:45. That's 18 minutes and 30 seconds that LSU had the ball more than Alabama. On paper that would seem to translate to a certain LSU victory. Where/how did the Crimson Tide win this game? Basically, the Crimson Tide performed better in clutch situations than did LSU. When the Tide needed to step it up to win, they did. LSU went for it on 4th down twice, and were stopped twice. Alabama did not go for it on 4th down, which in this game seems to have been the smarter decision. The Crimson Tide also won the penalty battle, giving up only 15 yards on 1 penalty, where LSU gave up 51 yards on 7 penalties. Lastly, there is no question that Alabama had superior play-calling. LSU had some downright unwise calls made in the 4th quarter that were very costly. Better disciplined players and smarter play-calling could very well have been the deciding factors in this close, 4-point game.

This game seemed to bring out the best performance in many of the athletes involved. For example, Zach Mettenberger had been floundering all season for LSU. In this game, he put up 298 yards and 1 touchdown with 0 interceptions against

Alabama's strong defense, truly one of the best defenses in all of college football. Something about facing the Crimson Tide lit a spark inside Mettenberger because he knew he needed to seriously step up his game for LSU to have any chance of winning. He did, but it still wasn't enough to overcome Alabama, who also rose to the occasion.

A.J. McCarron threw for 165 yards and 1 touchdown with no interceptions, which were some of his lowest numbers of the year. He also had his lowest completion percentage this far into the season of 51.85, his worst performance since the first game against Michigan. It is important to note that LSU's defense was strong and provided the toughest competition for the Alabama offense to date. Scoring 21 points on LSU was no easy feat, and that had only been done by 1 other team so far that year. On another front, McCarron did take the game into his own hands, running 3 times, including his touchdown run.

Alabama beat LSU by 4 points, which was much closer than the next-best opponent, who was Ole Miss, who lost by 19 points. It was a one-score game at the end, and that's something that no one had previously pushed Alabama to.

Alabama proved several things in this victory. First of all, they beat a worthy opponent, even more so a rival on the road in *Death Valley*. Secondly, they proved A.J. McCarron was the type of athlete who could lead his team to victory after being behind in points. That's a trait that many collegiate athletes lack. It's one thing to win when you're up. It's something else to perform under the pressure of the ticking clock while being down to a worthy challenger. Thirdly, Nick Saban demonstrated his superior coaching abilities again (even though he honestly had nothing to prove). While Les Miles was criticized for making several ridiculous and costly bad calls in the fourth quarter, Saban did not get rattled and made better decisions than his opposing coach. That is an element that championship teams need to have. Based on LSU's refusal to try something different while being pummeled in the 2012 BCS Championship Game and the poor calls in this game, it seems to be something that Les Miles, as great of a coach as he is, should pay more attention to – stable play calling in key games against great teams like the Crimson Tide.

TEAM LEADERS

Passing

A.J. McCarron #10
165 Yards, 1 Touchdown, 0 Interceptions
(14/27, 51.85 Comp %)

Rushing

Eddie Lacy #42
83 Yards on 11 Carries
7.55 Yards per Carry
1 Touchdown

T.J. Yeldon #4
76 Yards on 11 Carries
6.91 Yards per Carry
0 Touchdowns

A.J. McCarron #10
7 Yards on 3 Carries
2.33 Yards per Carry
1 Touchdown

Receiving

Kevin Norwood #83
62 Yards on 5 Receptions
12.4 Yards per Reception
0 Touchdowns

Christion Jones #22
40 Yards on 4 Receptions
10 Yards per Reception
0 Touchdowns

T.J. Yeldon #4
28 Yards on 1 Reception
28 Yards per Carry
1 Touchdown

Kicking

Jeremy Shelley #5
3 Points Total
0/0 Field Goals
3/3 Extra Points

Interceptions

None

THE BOTTOM LINE

9 - 0

GAME 10

November 10, 2012
Bryant-Denny Stadium – Tuscaloosa, AL

Teams	1st	2nd	3rd	4th	Total
#15 Texas A&M	20	0	0	9	29
#1 Alabama	0	14	3	7	24

GAME SUMMARY

Coming off back-to-back victories over #11 Mississippi State and #5 LSU, no one was expecting the Crimson Tide to lose to #15 Texas A&M. While Texas A&M was no slouch, they were a higher ranked team than their previous 2 opponents, and theoretically would not be as difficult of a challenge. That's where theory ends, and it's why the games, and not statistics, decide winners.

The Texas A&M Aggies may have only had a record of 7-2 (4-2 in the SEC) coming into this game, but they had a secret weapon in #2, freshman quarterback Johnny Manziel, aka Johnny Football. After all, at season's end, he became the first freshman to ever win the Heisman Trophy.

Let's face it: if a team was going to have any chance against the incredible 2012 Crimson Tide defense, they needed to have one heck of a quarterback. The only other serious threat to Alabama this season was LSU, when their there-to-for mediocre quarterback Mettenberger was having an amazingly incredible game, far beyond his previous performances. In a sense, the stars lined up for that to have even been a close game.

So what did Johnny Manziel do to lead his team to victory against the #1 Alabama Crimson Tide? He spurred them early on to jump out ahead of Alabama with a 3-touchdown lead. That was the largest lead anyone held over Alabama. Getting 3 touchdowns in a game against the Crimson Tide would have been an accomplishment. Getting 3 of them in the 1st quarter was simply shocking.

Manziel threw for 253 yards and 2 touchdowns with 0 interceptions. If that weren't enough, Manziel also rushed for 92 yards on his own, making himself the top rusher on his team, and tying Eddie Lacy for being the top rusher in the entire game. That's an amazing performance.

However, what speaks volumes for the quality of the 2012 Alabama Crimson Tide is that this amazing performance only resulted in beating the Tide by 5 points. After all of that offense by the Aggies, Alabama still came within one score of winning that game.

A.J. McCarron, while excelling at getting his team back in this game after quickly getting down by 20 unanswered points, had a mixed overall performance. McCarron who went the first 9 games of the season without a single interception, threw 2 away in this game. Arguably either one of them could have been the game-winning score, but it is probably a bit ridiculous for blaming a quarterback for having 2 interceptions in 10 games. It's hard to ask for more than that.

McCarron threw for 309 yards, which is fantastic. He threw for 1 touchdown, but as said above, gave up 2 interceptions. His completion percentage was 61.7, 10 points higher than it was in the previous victory over LSU, but about 10 points lower than his better performances. Still, Alabama won the passing game with 309 versus the Aggies' 253 yards.

But, in addition to the 2 interceptions, the Tide also lost a fumble. When you lose the turnover battle 3-0, you typically lose the game, no matter who your opponent may be.

Also in uncharacteristic fashion, Alabama lost the penalty war, committing 6 penalties for 56 yards compared to their opponents who committed 4 penalties for 26 yards.

Once again, the kicking game was flawless with Jeremy Shelley hitting 1/1 field goals and 3/3 extra points.

Despite the heartbreaking loss, that at the time could have ruined the Crimson Tide's national championship hopes, it was the second week in a row that Alabama showed great heart and determination in fighting back when they were down on the scoreboard. This was something that critics questioned earlier in the season, and even in this one loss, Alabama proved them wrong.

Team Leaders

Passing

A.J. McCarron #10
309 Yards, 1 Touchdown, 2 Interceptions
(21/34, 61.7 Comp %)

Rushing

Eddie Lacy #42
92 Yards on 16 Carries
5.75 Yards per Carry
1 Touchdown

T.J. Yeldon #4
29 Yards on 10 Carries
2.9 Yards per Carry
1 Touchdown

Receiving

Amari Cooper #9
136 Yards on 6 Receptions
22.67 Yards per Reception
1 Touchdown

Kenny Bell #7
73 Yards on 3 Receptions
24.33 Yards per Reception
0 Touchdowns

Eddie Lacy #42
35 Yards on 4 Receptions
8.75 Yards per Reception
0 Touchdowns

Christion Jones #22
21 Yards on 3 Receptions
7 Yards per Reception
0 Touchdowns

Kicking

Jeremy Shelley #5
6 Points Total
1/1 Field Goals
3/3 Extra Points

Interceptions

None

THE BOTTOM LINE

9 - 1

GAME 11

November 17, 2012
Bryant-Denny Stadium – Tuscaloosa, AL

Teams	1st	2nd	3rd	4th	Total
W Carolina	0	0	0	0	**0**
#4 Alabama	21	21	7	0	**49**

GAME SUMMARY

After the previous week's upset loss to the Texas A&M Aggies and possibly having lost their chance to make it to the national championship game, it was expected that the Crimson Tide would come out angry and with something to prove against the lowly, unranked, 1-9 West Carolina Catamounts, who were on a 9-game losing streak, having not won a single game since their season opener.

Because of the previous week's loss, Alabama was ranked down to #4, a decline of which some fans thought to be quite unfair, considering it was only a loss by 5 points to a #15 team. Having been #1 since the second game of the season, this undoubtedly lit a fire underneath the Crimson Tide.

What ensued was a true slaughter. 49-0, with 42 of those points scored by the half is a blowout of a blowout. If Alabama wanted to show the world that they were still in the fight for the national title, they certainly did so before the first 2 quarters were over.

460 yards of Crimson Tide total offense versus 163 total yards of offense from the Catamounts really tells the entire story of this game.

This was truly a running game. A.J. McCarron was perfect, throwing 6 completions on 6 passes for 133 yards and 1 touchdown. But, there were only 8 total receptions for the team on the day. However, there were 40 rushing plays, accounting for a whopping 300+ yards and 5 rushing touchdowns, including 3 TDs by Eddie Lacy alone.

The only thing even in this entire game was the turnover battle. Both teams lost a fumble with no interceptions. Everything else was strictly a no-contest.

By the way, if anyone is interested in finding out exactly what a catamount is, I've done the legwork for you. A catamount is a broad term for wild cats, such as bobcats, cougars, or lynxes *(And, yes, I checked that the plural of lynx is lynxes. Lynx is also an equally acceptable plural of lynx)*. These types of wild cats can be found in the Appalachian Mountains in the vicinity of Western Carolina University, so it is a logical choice for their mascot, as odd as the word may sound.

TEAM LEADERS

Passing

A.J. McCarron #10
133 Yards, 1 Touchdown, 0 Interceptions
(6/6, 100 Comp %)

Rushing

Eddie Lacy #42
99 Yards on 10 Carries
9.9 Yards per Carry
3 Touchdowns

Blake Sims #6
70 Yards on 8 Carries
8.75 Yards per Carry
1 Touchdown

T.J. Yeldon #4
55 Yards on 7 Carries
7.86 Yards per Carry
1 Touchdown

Brent Calloway #21
52 Yards on 7 Carries
7.43 Yards per Carry
0 Touchdowns

Receiving

Amari Cooper #9
50 Yards on 2 Receptions
25 Yards per Reception
0 Touchdowns

Kenny Bell #7
34 Yards on 1 Reception
34 Yards per Reception
0 Touchdowns

Christion Jones #22
29 Yards on 1 Reception
29 Yards per Reception
1 Touchdown

Kicking

Jeremy Shelley #5
7 Points Total
0/0 Field Goals
7/7 Extra Points

Interceptions

None

THE BOTTOM LINE

10 - 1

GAME 12

November 24, 2012
Bryant-Denny Stadium – Tuscaloosa, AL

Teams	1st	2nd	3rd	4th	Total
Auburn	0	0	0	0	0
#2 Alabama	14	28	7	0	49

GAME SUMMARY

Auburn, a once-competitive SEC team, was having a miserable year, eventually ending its season 3-9 (0-8 in the SEC. Yeah, that's right: winless in all 8 of its SEC games). Everyone knew this one was going to be ugly, and it ended up being a 49-point shutout. Yes, if you're following close that's the same staggering score from the previous week versus West Carolina University.

Based on last week's games, Alabama moved from #4 up to #2 coming into this game.

A.J. McCarron got some exercise in this one, throwing for 4 touchdowns on 216 yards with 0 interceptions.

The game is an easy one to describe by just looking at Alabama's 483 yards of total offense versus Auburn's 163. In addition to that, Alabama won the turnover war, 3-1. When you get 3 times more turnovers than you give up and you earn 3 times more yards on offense than your opponent, you can pretty much put the mark in your team's win column without ever even looking at the scoreboard.

TEAM LEADERS

Passing

A.J. McCarron #10
216 Yards, 4 Touchdowns, 0 Interceptions
(15/21, 71.42 Comp %)

Rushing

Eddie Lacy #42
131 Yards on 18 Carries
7.28 Yards per Carry
2 Touchdowns

Kenyan Drake #17
67 Yards on 10 Carries
6.7 Yards per Carry
0 Touchdowns

T.J. Yeldon #4
38 Yards on 8 Carries
4.75 Yards per Carry
1 Touchdown

Receiving

Amari Cooper #9
109 Yards on 5 Receptions
21.8 Yards per Reception
2 Touchdowns

Kevin Norwood #83
65 Yards on 5 Receptions
13 Yards per Reception
2 Touchdowns

Christion Jones #22
22 Yards on 3 Receptions
7.33 Yards per Reception
0 Touchdowns

Kicking

Jeremy Shelley #5
7 Points Total
0/0 Field Goals
7/7 Extra Points

Interceptions

Ha'Sean Clinton-Dix #6
1 Interception

Robert Lester #37
1 Interception

THE BOTTOM LINE

11 - 1

GAME 13

SEC Championship Game

December 1, 2012
Georgia Dome – Atlanta, GA

Teams	1st	2nd	3rd	4th	Total
#3 Georgia	0	7	14	7	**28**
#2 Alabama	0	10	8	14	**32**

GAME SUMMARY

Other than the loss to Texas A&M, this was the closest contest Alabama had allowed since the 4-point game with LSU. Both teams were 11-1 overall, but Gerogia had a better SEC record of 7-0 to Alabama's 6-1.

McCarron had a mediocre day throwing for 162 yards on 13 of 21 passes for 1 touchdown and 1 interception.

The running game was responsible for most of the team's points, with 2 rushing touchdowns from Eddie Lacy and 1 more from T.J. Yeldon. All in all, the Crimson Tide's rushing game accounted for 350 yards on 51 carries. That's very impressive.

Alabama lost the turnover battle 2-1 (1 fumble and 1 interception). However, they won the penalty war with only 2 penalties for 15 yards versus Georgia's 7 penalties for 64 yards.

If one only looked at total yards, it would seem this game should not have been anywhere near as close as it was. Alabama earned 512 total offensive yards versus Georgia's 394 yards. Both teams were identical on 3rd down efficiency with 4 of 12. Georgia was the only team to go for it on 4th down, and they were successful on their one attempt to do so.

The end of the game was a scary one for Alabama fans as with 1:08 second left on the clock, Georgia quarterback, Aaron Murray drove his team all the way 80 yards down field to Alabama's 5-yard line.

Alabama held onto the win by 4 points as the clock ran out on Georgia's cinematic run. The game was regarded as an exciting classic by fans and sports writers.

TEAM LEADERS

Passing

A.J. McCarron #10
162 Yards, 1 Touchdown, 1 Interception
(13/21, 69.90 Comp %)

Rushing

Eddie Lacy #42
181 Yards on 20 Carries
9.05 Yards per Carry
2 Touchdowns

T.J. Yeldon #4
153 Yards on 25 Carries
6.12 Yards per Carry
1 Touchdown

Receiving

Amari Cooper #9
128 Yards on 8 Receptions
16 Yards per Reception
1 Touchdown

Christion Jones #22
22 Yards on 1 Receptions
22 Yards per Reception
0 Touchdowns

Eddie Lacy #42
7 Yards on 2 Receptions
3.5 Yards per Reception
0 Touchdowns

Kicking

Jeremy Shelley #5
6 Points Total
1/1 Field Goals
3/3 Extra Points

Cade Foster #43
0 Points Total
0/1 Field Goals
0/0 Extra Points

Interceptions

Ha'Sean Clinton-Dix #6
1 Interception

Dan Fathow 68

THE BOTTOM LINE

12 - 1

SEC CHAMPIONS

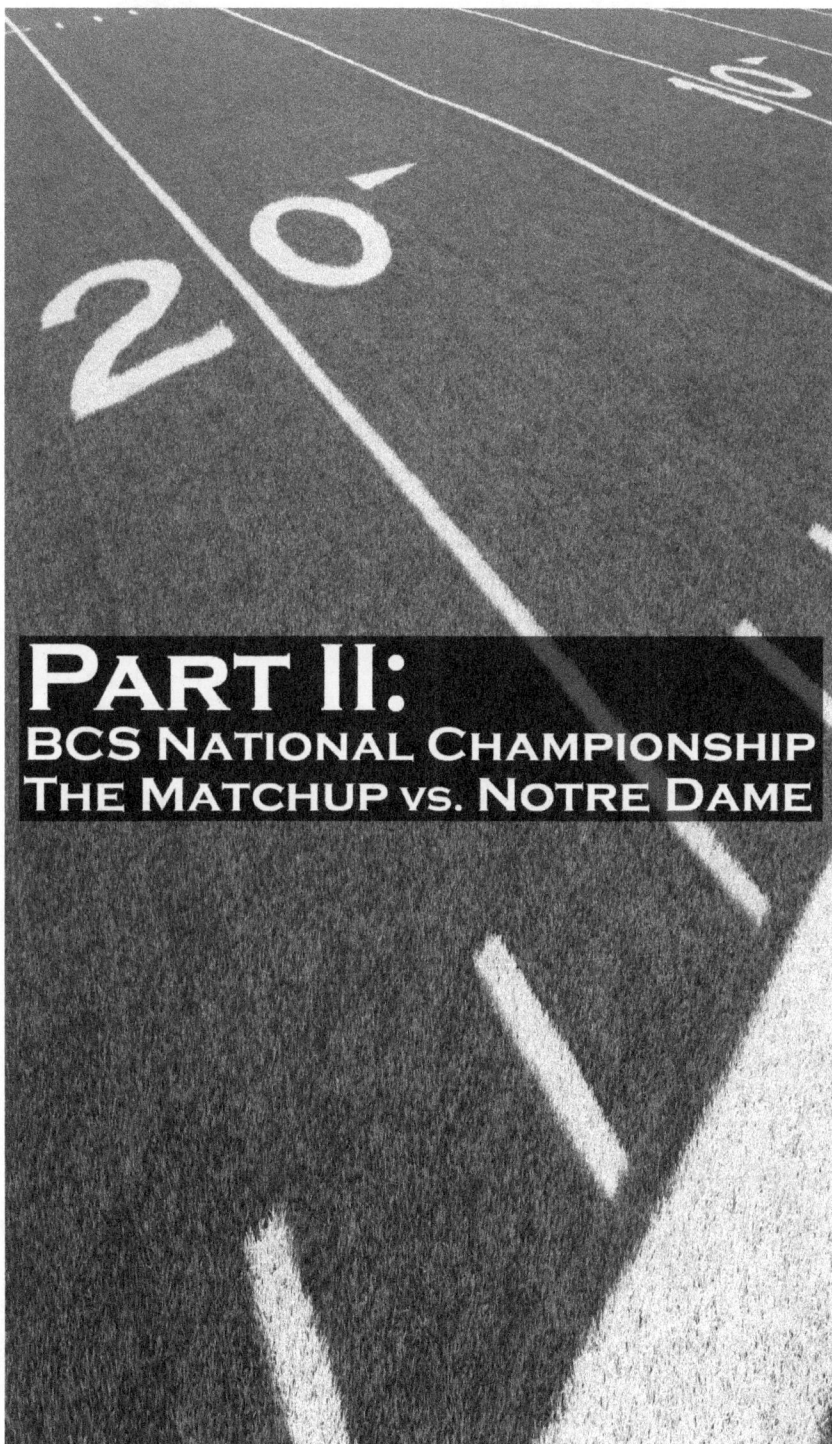

PART II:
BCS NATIONAL CHAMPIONSHIP
THE MATCHUP vs. NOTRE DAME

Momentum, Advantages, & Minutiae

Wear & Tear

Alabama will have played 13 games going into the BCS Title Game on Monday, January 7, 2013, and they will have last played against Georgia in the SEC Championship on December 1st.

Notre Dame will have only played 12 games going into the BCS Title Game on January 7, 2013, and they will have last played against USC on November 24th.

What does this mean in relation to the BCS Championship Game?

Alabama will have played one more game than Alabama, having put their players through more wear and tear.

Advantage: Notre Dame

Time Off - Rust Factor VS Rest Factor

Notre Dame will have had 44 days off compared to Alabama's 37 Days off. So, Notre Dame has had one more week off than Alabama. More time off is not always a good thing. Whether the bye week in the NFL is beneficial or harmful has long been a debate among fans and commentators.

On advancednflstats.com, Denis O'Regan put together one of the best studies on this issue. After crunching a ton of numbers that are a bit irrelevant to this college football discussion, he came up with a conclusion that may be very relevant to the BCS Championship Game:

"Conclusion.

Favoured teams going on the road after a bye week appear to overperform by almost a field goal. This effect is largely absent in all other types of matchups."

(Denis O'Regan - Writer, Ed Anthony – Editor,
October 31, 2009
http://community.advancednflstats.com/2009/10/bye-weeks.html)

Okay, so that's an in-depth analysis of NFL teams' performances following a bye week. What does that have to do with the BCS Championship Game? Well, maybe nothing. Even if statistics are very strongly against something from happening in the sports world, there is a first time for everything, and there are no statistics that can prevent an athlete or a team to win in an underdog position. This very fact is probably what keeps us watching sports year after year. It's the chance that heart, determination, and hard work can make a champion out of someone that the world underestimated. And, by the same token, a tremendously talented team can lose to anyone if they grow overconfident, complacent, or take their opponent too lightly.

Okay, okay, so that's enough waxing poetic about the valor of sports. What does Mr. O'Regan's study mean for the BCS Championship Game?

Depending on where you look, Alabama is favored to win by between 8-10 points, even though Notre Dame is undefeated. The game is being held in Miami, FL, so both teams count as road teams in this scenario. If O'Regan's statistics hold true in the BCS title game, it would mean Alabama would score 3 more points than the expected spread predicts. If the experts are right, Alabama wins. In Notre Dame's defense, they have consistently been wrong about the Fighting Irish all year.

Advantage: *a slight maybe to Alabama*

TEAM PASSING STATISTICS

TEAM	Comp	Attempts	Comp %	Yards	TDs	Inter-ceptions
Alabama	199	300	66.3	2,788	27	3
Notre Dame	205	352	58.2	2,626	13	7

The obvious big difference in the passing department is that Alabama has double the touchdowns with less than half the interceptions. The advantage here obviously lies with the Crimson Tide.

TEAM RUSHING STATISTICS

TEAM	Carries	Yards	Average	Touchdowns
Alabama	525	2,920	5.6 Yards	35
Notre Dame	487	2,430	5 Yards	22

On one hand the rushing numbers are similar. Alabama has about 500 more yards, but they also took an extra 38 carries to get them. The yards per carry are close with Alabama earning 0.6 more yards per carry than Notre Dame. The big difference here is that Alabama picked up 13 more rushing touchdowns than the Fighting Irish during the regular season.

TEAM KICKING STATISTICS

TEAM	Extra Points	Extra Point %	Field Goals	Field Goal %	Total Points
Alabama	63	100	15	75	108
Notre Dame	31	94	24	75	103

The kicking game is probably the most balanced element between both teams. Alabama has a perfect extra point percentage, while Notre Dame has a 94% accuracy. On field goals, both teams have a 75% accuracy, but Notre Dame kicked 9 more field goals than Alabama. The total kicking points are nearly identical with Alabama at 108 and Notre Dame at 103. The kicking edge seems to lie a little more with Notre Dame being that Notre Dame kicked 60% more field goals than Alabama. Field goals will likely have more of an impact on a national title win than extra points.

TEAM DEFENSIVE TURNOVERS

TEAM	Interceptions	Fumbles
Alabama	17	4
Notre Dame	16	2

The defensive turnovers are nearly identical too, both teams having incredible defenses. Alabama has one more interception and two more fumbles, but it's too close to call to say either team has a true advantage here. Both teams have relied on their solid defenses and great turnover rates all year round, and they will surely play a vital role in deciding the winner of the 2013 BCS National Championship Game.

QUARTERBACK MATCHUP

McCARRON VS. GOLSON

By the numbers:

A.J. McCARRON

Year	CMP	ATT	YDS	CMP%	TD	INT
2012	191	286	2669	66.8	26	3
2011	219	328	2634	66.8	16	5
2010	30	48	389	62.5	3	0

A.J. GOLSON

Year	CMP	ATT	YDS	CMP%	TD	INT
2012	166	282	2135	58.9	11	5

Even though Everett Golson has led Notre Dame through a fantastic season, AJ McCarron leads Golson in passing yards, completion percentage, touchdowns, and a far superior touchdown to interception ratio. While McCarron threw 8.67 touchdowns for every interception, Golson only threw 2.2 touchdowns for every interception. So McCarron threw nearly 4 times as many touchdowns per interception as his competitor during the regular season leading up to the BCS

Title Game. Turnovers often decide football games; whether Golson can improve on these numbers or not in the big game could be the deciding factor.

EXPERIENCE

2012 was Everett Golson's first year as a starter, and during that year, he split a lot of games with Tommy Rees. A.J. McCarron has been the Crimson Tide's quarterback for 3 years, as the full-time starter the last 2 of those.

Besides the number of snaps and years of experience, there is also big game experience. Many players have found it difficult to perform in championship games in the same manner and at the same level as they had done all season. Press and media hoopla can unnerve many otherwise cool customers. Everett Golson, in his first year as a starter, has no previous experience in championship game pressure.

On the other hand, A.J. McCarron has already won a BCS Championship in 2012 against an undefeated LSU Tigers team, in New Orleans no less. In this game, McCarron led the Crimson Tide to a 21-0 victory while throwing for 234 yards on 23 completions on 34 attempts. In that game, McCarron did not throw a single interception.

If there is a criticism to be made of McCarron's performance in that victory, it is that he did not throw a single touchdown pass against a disoriented and poorly-performing LSU team. All of Alabama's points against LSU came in the form of 5 field goals by Jeremy Shelley and one rushing touchdown by Trent Richardson. It is important to note that McCarron was without his top receiver, Marquis Maze, who left the field with a leg injury in the first quarter and was unable to return. Perhaps there would have been a McCarron to Maze touchdown pass if not for the injury. Regardless, not only has McCarron faced this pressure, but he has overcome it and excelled in spite of it.

So, Golson has not been to the big game before and neither does he have the experience of A.J. McCarron in the regular season. However, the entire 2012 season has been a series of challenges that Golson has risen to and met head on. Throughout the course of the season, Everett Golson has had to fight for his position as a starter against more experienced quarterback Tommy Rees. He's had to overcome an injury, and he's had to deal with the pressure of leading an underdog Notre Dame team through an undefeated season, including beating several ranked teams. It seemed every week the media and sports analysts were predicting Notre Dame's charmed winning streak would come to end, but it never did. Somehow, someway Golson led his team to victory, doing whatever it took in each specific situation for the Fighting Irish to get a mark in the win column. Overcoming higher-ranked teams and adversity has been no problem for Golson all season, so it's hard to count him out because he's facing a strong defense and a quarterback with more experience who has already won a national championship. It would seem the entire 2012 season was a preparation for Golson to meet this last challenge.

So, who's going to have the better day? Who is going to win the championship for their team?

Well, winning the championship is absolutely a team effort, so it's a bit cheeky to say either quarterback has that power alone. However, it's undeniable that a great quarterback performance, especially one with zero turnovers, can help lead a team to victory. If you're going by the numbers alone, it's likely that McCarron will put up better stats and help put the Crimson Tide on top. If you're going by Golson's ability to accomplish whatever needed to be done to win, it's likely that Golson may perform better in the clutch, maybe enough to put the Fighting Irish on top. Golson is not likely to beat McCarron on stats, but it is likely that he'll deliver on key plays. The danger with Golson is that if this game follows the regular season stats, he may throw more interceptions, which can easily give the game away to a capable team like Alabama.

What's most likely to happen is that two great quarterbacks and team leaders will both have a great day, providing an exciting and memorable championship game.

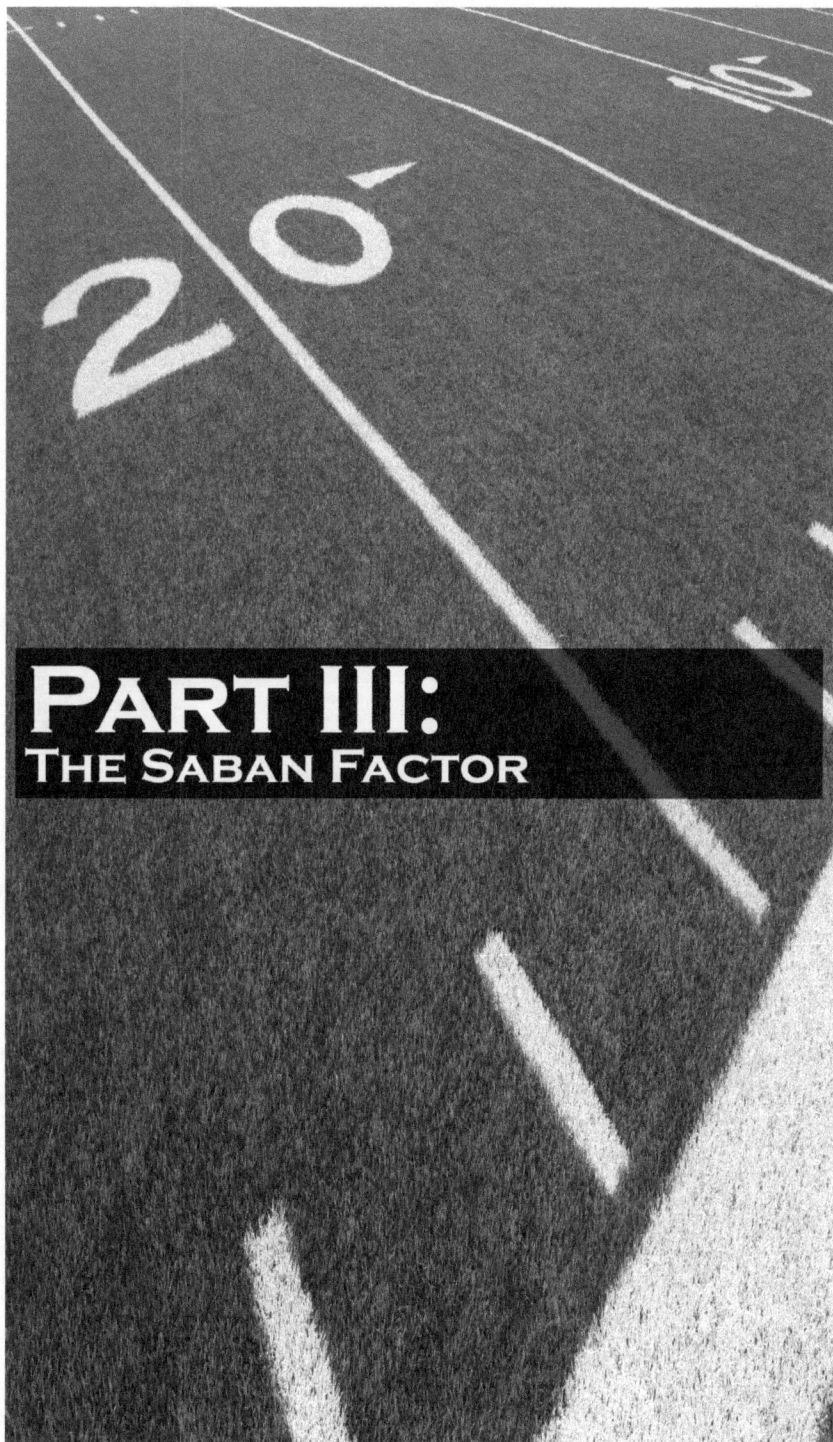

PART III:
THE SABAN FACTOR

THE SABAN FACTOR
AN OLD ENEMY & A NEW FRIEND TO THE CRIMSON TIDE

O kay, so the chapter title may be a little dramatic, but it does somewhat capture the long-standing relationship between Nick Saban and Alabama fans.

A little history…

Nick Saban took over head coaching duties at LSU from Gary DiNardo for the 2000 football season. Despite getting LSU fans' hopes up on several occasions, DiNardo could never get the Tigers into championship shape, and in his last year with the team, he led them to an uninspired 3-8 record.

In just his first year as head coach, Saban improved LSU's record to 8-4. He basically flipped their record around, turning the Tigers from a team that lost nearly three times as much as they won into a team that won twice as much as they lost.

In his second year in Baton Rouge, Saban coached LSU to win an SEC championship. In only two years' time, the Tigers went from a 3-8 record to SEC Champions. That's pretty amazing.

The crowning achievement of Saban's tenure at LSU was obviously the 2003 shared National Championship.

Saban stayed on for one more year following the national championship, leading the Tigers to a 9-3 season, which included a heart-wrenching 1-point loss to Auburn.

When Saban left college football to coach in the NFL's 2005 season, he did not leave LSU for rival Alabama. He became the head coach of the Miami Dolphins. The last two sentences are extremely obvious, but they deserve repeating, because some people seem to think that Saban did indeed leave LSU for Alabama, and that is downright silly. The simple truth is that while Saban eventually left the Miami Dolphins to become Alabama's head coach, his job was not guaranteed with the Dolphins' disappointing 6-10 2006 Season. Any NFL coach with a 6-10 record is in danger of losing his job, especially a high profile coach who has not performed up to expectations. If the 2007 season did not show significant improvement for the Dolphins, Saban would very likely have been fired, harming both his reputation and the salary that he could receive elsewhere. For the record, the 2007 Dolphins were plagued with problems on and off the field which led to a miserable 1-15 season. Three Dolphins players were arrested that year, and one can only speculate if these personnel problems were an additional motivation for Saban to seek a new position. Maybe Saban saw the trouble brewing and decided to get out ahead of time, or maybe he honestly felt that he did not deliver the performance he was paid for and decided it was best for the team to go on without him. Either way, it seems to have been the smartest decision for all involved.

An SEC Coach taking a head coaching position at a rival school is big news, but it's not industrial espionage either. In January of 2007, Alabama needed a coach, and Saban needed/wanted a new coaching job. Seeking work in one's qualified field is not a malicious act. If LSU had offered Saban his job back for the same money that Alabama offered and Saban had then refused LSU to go to Alabama, then, one could argue ill will and a lack of loyalty, but that didn't happen. The man wanted to return to college football and took the best position available at the time.

Since taking the position as head coach of the Alabama Crimson Tide, Nick Saban has enjoyed success that few collegiate coaches will ever know.

In 2005, Nick Saban wrote *How Good Do You Want to Be?: A Champion's Tips on How to Lead and Succeed at Work and in Life* with the help of co-author Brian Curtis. At the time of this pressing, the book is currently available through Ballantine Books. Be warned that although the book contains a lot of great information and it now has an Alabama cover, it focuses on his tenure at LSU, which makes sense since the book was written before his tenure at Alabama started. The original cover did have Saban in purple and gold. Besides talking about football, the book focuses on what Saban considers to be the key elements to success in any field: organization, motivation, ethics, and being very honest about your strengths and weaknesses. So, there is a lot more in the book than purple and gold celebrating.

At the end of the 2012 regular season, Nick Saban has led his Crimson Tide to a back-to-back BCS National Championship Game, earning the rare opportunity to repeat as the recognized greatest team in college football. With that potential win, Saban will have also won bowl games a staggering 4 years in a row, and 5 wins in 6 bowl appearances in his time with Alabama.

Possibly Saban's greatest accomplishment would be winning the BCS National Championship 3 times in 4 years. He's already done it 2 times in 3 years.

Nick Saban Collegiate Head Coaching Record – All Teams

Season	College	Record	Bowl Game
1990	Toledo	09-02	N/A
1995	Michigan State	06-05-01	*LOSS – Independence Bowl*
1996	Michigan State	06-06	*LOSS – Sun Bowl*
1997	Michigan State	07-05	*LOSS – Aloha Bowl*
1998	Michigan State	06-06	
1999	Michigan State	09-02	
2000	LSU	08-04	**WIN – Peach Bowl**
2001	LSU	10-03	**WIN – Sugar Bowl**
2002	LSU	08-05	*LOSS – Cotton Bowl*
2003	LSU	13-01	**WIN – Sugar Bowl**
2004	LSU	09-03	*LOSS – Capital One Bowl*
2007	Alabama	07-06 (02-06)	**WIN - Independence Bowl**
2008	Alabama	12-02	*LOSS – Sugar Bowl*
2009	Alabama	14-00	**WIN - BCS Championship Game**
2010	Alabama	10-03	**WIN – Capital One Bowl**
2011	Alabama	12-01	**WIN – BCS Championship Game**
2012	Alabama	13-1	BCS (TBD)
ALL	**ALL**	**158-55-01**	07-06 in Bowl Games
ALL	**Adjusted by NCAA**	**153-55-01**	

Nick Saban Michigan State Head Coaching Record

Seasons	College	Record	Win %	Bowl Game Record
1995-1999	Michigan State	34-24	58.62 %	0-3

Nick Saban LSU Head Coaching Record

Seasons	College	Record	Win %	Bowl Game Record
2000-2004	LSU	48-16	75 %	3-2

Nick Saban Alabama Head Coaching Record

Seasons	College	Record	Win %	Bowl Game Record
2007-2012	Alabama	67-13	83.75 %	4-1 (not including 2013 BCS)

Clearly Nick Saban has had a successful career, but his best years have certainly been with the Alabama Crimson Tide, which have produced 3 trips to the BCS Championship Game, a 4-1 bowl game record, 67 wins, and an 83.75% win percentage. If you ignore his first year in Alabama that was a little rocky (while still producing a trip and win to the Independence Bowl), Saban-coached Alabama teams have won at least 10 games every year with a win percentage of 89.55%. That's hard to beat.

DAN FATHOW 86

ALABAMA CRIMSON TIDE PLAYERS BY THE NUMBERS

Number	Name	Position	Height	Weight	Year
1	Dee Hart	RB	5'9"	190	FR
2	DeAndrew White	WR	6'1"	185	SO
3	Sunseri, Vinnie	DB	6'1"	215	SO
4	T.J. Yeldon	RB	6'2"	216	FR
5	Chris Black	WR	5'11"	178	FR
5	Jeremy Shelley	K	5'10"	165	SR
6	Ha'Sean Clinton-Dix	DB	6'1"	209	SO
6	Blake Sims	RB	6'1"	212	SO
7	Ryan Anderson	LB	6'2"	252	FR
7	Kenny Bell	WR	6'1"	180	JR
8	Cyrus Jones	WR	5'10"	192	FR
8	Jeoffrey Pagan	DL	6'4"	285	SO
9	Amari Cooper	WR	6'1"	198	FR
10	John Fulton	DB	6'1"	187	JR

10	AJ McCarron	QB	6'4"	210	JR
11	Alec Morris	QB	6'3"	225	FR
11	Tana Patrick	LB	6'3"	236	JR
12	Phillip Ely	QB	6'1"	198	FR
13	Deion Belue	DB	5'11"	179	JR
13	Ty Reed	QB	6'1"	190	JR
14	Edward Aldag	QB	6'1"	183	FR
15	Eddie Williams	WR	6'3	204	FR
16	Bradley Sylve	DB	5'11	178	FR
17	Caleb Castille	DB	5'11	170	SO
17	Kenyan Drake	RB	6'1	204	FR
17	Parker Philpot	DB	5'10	180	JR
18	Levi Cook	DB	5'10	190	SR
18	Reggie Ragland	LB	6'2	247	FR
18	Nick Williams	WR	5'10	185	JR
19	Jonathan Atchison	LB	6'3	236	JR

2012 ALABAMA CRIMSON TIDE 89

19	Dustin Ellison	QB	6'1	180	SO
20	Nathan McAlister	WR	5'11	165	SR
20	Jarrick Williams	DB	6'1	212	JR
21	Brent Calloway	LB	6'1	217	FR
21	Bryson Moultry	DB	6'0	185	SO
21	Ranzell Watkins	DB	5'9	172	JR
22	Hunter Bush	DB	5'11	195	SR
22	Christion Jones	WR	5'11	185	SO
23	Taylor Morton	DB	5'11"	185	SO
23	Jabriel Washington	DB	5'11"	183	FR
24	Geno Smith	DB	6'1"	182	FR
25	Dillon Lee	LB	6'4"	240	FR
26	Landon Collins	DB	6'1"	202	FR
27	Nick Perry	DB	6'1"	208	JR
28	Dee Milliner	DB	6'1"	199	JR
29	Cody Mandell	P	6'4"	202	JR

30	Denzel Devall	LB	6'2"	243	FR
31	Jerrod Bierbower	DB	6'1"	185	SO
31	Kelly Johnson	TE	6'3"	230	SR
32	C.J. Mosley	LB	6'2"	232	JR
32	Trey Roberts	RB	6'1"	189	FR
33	Trey DePriest	LB	6'2"	245	SO
33	Marcus Polk	WR	5'8"	180	SO
34	Ben Howell	RB	5'9"	194	SR
34	Tyler Owens	LB	6'1"	220	SO
35	Nico Johnson	LB	6'3"	245	SR
36	Tyler Hayes	LB	6'2"	210	FR
37	Robert Lester	DB	6'2	210	SR
40	Spencer Duncan	RB	6'2	230	SO
41	Kurt Freitag	TE	6'4	240	FR
42	Adrian Hubbard	LB	6'6	248	SO
42	Eddie Lacy	RB	6'1	220	JR

43	Cade Foster	K	6'1	218	JR
44	LaMichael Fanning	DL	6'7	298	FR
45	Jalston Fowler	RB	6'1	242	JR
46	Michael Nysewander	TE	6'1	230	SO
46	Wilson Whorton	P	5'10	175	SO
47	Xzavier Dickson	LB	6'3	262	SO
47	Corey McCarron	TE	6'2	240	SO
48	Rowdy Harrell	LB	6'1	221	SR
49	Ed Stinson	DL	6'4	282	JR
50	Alphonse Taylor	DL	6'5	340	FR
51	Wilson Love	DL	6'3	281	FR
51	Carson Tinker	LS	6'1	220	SR
52	MK Taylor	LS	5'10	210	JR
52	Dalvin Tomlinson	DL	6'2	266	FR
53	Anthony Orr	DL	6'4"	258	SO
54	Russell Raines	OL	6'2"	277	JR

54	Jesse Williams	DL	6'4"	320	SR
55	Josh Dickerson	LB	6'1"	238	SO
56	William Ming	DL	6'3"	283	JR
57	Aaron Joiner	OL	6'2"	265	SR
57	D.J. Pettway	DL	6'2"	285	FR
58	Brandon Greene	OL	6'5"	292	FR
59	Harold Nicholson	OL	6'5"	292	SO
61	Anthony Steen	OL	6'3"	303	JR
62	Brandon Ivory	DL	6'4"	315	SO
63	Kellen Williams	OL	6'3"	303	JR
64	Michael Newsome	DL	6'2"	250	SO
65	Chance Warmack	OL	6'3"	320	SR
67	Alex Shine	OL	6'3"	300	FR
68	Isaac Luatua	OL	6'2"	313	FR
69	Paul Waldrop	OL	6'4"	267	FR
70	Ryan Kelly	OL	6'5	288	FR

71	Cyrus Kouandjio	OL	6'6	311	SO
74	Caleb Gulledge	OL	6'4	280	FR
75	Barrett Jones	OL	6'5	302	SR
76	D.J. Fluker	OL	6'6	335	JR
77	Arie Kouandjio	OL	6'5	310	SO
78	Chad Lindsay	OL	6'2	290	SO
79	Austin Shepherd	OL	6'5	312	SO
80	Marvin Shinn	WR	6'3	198	FR
81	Danny Woodson	WR	6'1	195	FR
82	Harrison Jones	TE	6'4	244	SO
83	Kevin Norwood	WR	6'2	195	JR
84	Brian Vogler	TE	6'7	258	SO
85	Malcolm Faciane	TE	6'5	259	FR
85	Korren Kirven	DL	6'5	292	FR
87	Parker Barrineau	WR	6'1	175	SO
88	Josh Magee	WR	6'1	170	FR

89	Michael Williams	TE	6'6	269	SR
90	Quinton Dial	DL	6'6"	304	SR
92	Damion Square	DL	6'3"	286	SR
93	Chris Bonds	DL	6'4"	273	JR
94	Dakota Ball	DL	6'2"	295	FR
95	Darren Lake	DL	6'3"	315	FR
98	Dillon Drake	K	5'9"	175	SO
99	Adam Griffith	K	5'10"	174	FR

Notre Dame Fighting Irish Players by the Numbers

Number	Name	Position	Height	Weight	Year
1	Gunner Kiel	QB	6'4"	210	SO
2	Chris Brown	WR	6'2"	172	FR
2	Bennett Jackson	CB	6'1"	185	JR
3	Amir Carlisle	RB	5'10"	185	SO
4	George Atkinson III	RB	6'1"	210	SO
4	Eilar Hardy	S	5'11"	185	SO
5	Everett Golson	QB	6'1"	185	SO
5	Manti Te'o	LB	6'2"	255	SR
6	Theo Riddick	RB	5'11"	200	SR
6	KeiVarae Russell	CB	5'11"	182	FR
7	TJ Jones	WR	5'11"	190	JR
7	Stephon Tuitt	DE	6'6"	303	SO
8	Kendall Moore	LB	6'1"	242	JR
9	Louis Nix III	DL	6'3"	326	JR

9	Robby Toma	WR	5'9"	185	SR
10	DaVaris Daniels	WR	6'2"	190	SO
11	Tommy Rees	QB	6'2"	210	JR
11	Ishaq Williams	LB	6'5"	255	SO
12	Andrew Hendrix	QB	6'2"	220	JR
13	Danny Spond	LB	6'2"	248	JR
14	Luke Massa	WR	6'4"	225	JR
15	Dan McCarthy	S	6'2"	205	SR
16	Chris Badger	S	6'1"	193	FR
17	Charlie Fiessinger	QB	6'1"	185	SO
17	Zeke Motta	S	6'2"	215	SR
18	Ben Koyack	TE	6'5"	253	SO
19	Davonte' Neal	WR	5'9"	171	FR
20	Cierre Wood	RB	6'1"	215	SR
21	Jalen Brown	CB	6'1"	199	SO
22	Elijah Shumate	S	6'1"	198	FR

23	Lo Wood	CB	5'10"	195	JR
24	Chris Salvi	S	5'10"	190	SR
26	Jamoris Slaughter	S	6'1"	200	SR
27	Kyle Brindza	K	6'1"	225	SO
28	Austin Collinsworth	S	6'1"	202	JR
29	Nicky Baratti	S	6'1"	206	FR
30	Ben Councell	LB	6'5"	240	SO
31	John Turner	S	6'2"	207	FR
32	Will Mahone	RB	5'10"	211	FR
33	Cam McDaniel	CB	5'10"	195	SO
34	C.J. Prosise	S	6'2"	208	FR
35	Joe Romano	CB	5'9"	175	JR
35	Ben Turk	P	5'11"	186	SR
36	Will Salvi	CB	5'10"	176	SR
37	Eric Lee	WR	5'9"	180	SO
38	Nick Fitzpatrick	WR	5'8"	170	SR

38	Joe Schmidt	LB	6'1"	230	SO
39	Ryan Liebscher	WR	5'11"	205	JR
39	Jude Rhodes	P	5'10"	180	JR
40	Nick Tausch	K	6'1"	201	SR
41	Matthias Farley	S	5'11"	200	SO
42	Ernie Soto	S	5'9"	188	SO
43	Josh Atkinson	CB	5'11"	185	SO
44	Carlo Calabrese	LB	6'1"	245	SR
45	Romeo Okwara	LB	6'4"	239	FR
46	Josh Anderson	WR	5'9"	180	FR
46	Eamon McOsker	S	6'1"	200	FR
47	Connor Cavalaris	S	5'10"	194	SO
48	Dan Fox	LB	6'3"	240	SR
49	Blake Breslau	S	5'10"	185	SR
49	Tyler Plantz	RB	5'9"	202	JR
50	Chase Hounshell	DE	6'4"	275	SO

51	Bruce Heggie	C	6'5"	285	JR
52	Braxston Cave	C	6'3"	304	SR
53	Justin Utupo	DE	6'1"	258	JR
54	Kevin Walsh	LB	6'3"	220	SR
55	Prince Shembo	LB	6'2"	250	JR
56	Anthony Rabasa	LB	6'3"	240	SO
57	Mike Golic Jr.	C	6'3"	300	SR
59	Jarrett Grace	LB	6'3"	240	SO
60	Jordan Cowart	LS	6'2"	230	SR
61	Scott Daly	LS	6'2"	245	FR
62	Matt Tansey	OL	6'6"	270	SR
63	Grant Patton	DE	6'6"	256	SR
64	Tate Nichols	OT	6'8"	320	JR
65	Conor Hanratty	G	6'5"	305	SO
66	Chris Watt	G	6'3"	310	SR
67	Kevin Carr	DE	6'7"	325	JR

69	Tony Springmann	DL	6'6"	300	SO
70	Zack Martin	OT	6'4"	304	SR
71	Dennis Mahoney	OT	6'7"	294	SR
72	Nick Martin	OT	6'4"	290	SO
73	Dan Furlong	OL	6'7"	250	FR
74	Christian Lombard	G	6'5"	309	JR
75	Mark Harrell	OL	6'4"	287	FR
77	Matt Hegarty	C	6'5"	296	SO
78	Ronnie Stanley	OL	6'6"	304	FR
80	Tyler Eifert	TE	6'6"	251	SR
81	John Goodman	WR	6'3"	215	SR
82	Justin Ferguson	WR	6'2"	196	FR
82	Alex Welch	TE	6'4"	250	JR
83	Gerard Martinez	WR	6'1"	200	FR
84	Andre Smith	WR	6'2"	190	SO
85	Troy Niklas	TE	6'7"	260	SO

86	Arturo Martinez	DE	6'4"	250	JR
87	Daniel Smith	WR	6'4"	215	JR
88	Jake Golic	TE	6'4"	245	SR
89	Kapron Lewis-Moore	DE	6'4"	306	SR
91	Sheldon Day	DE	6'2"	286	FR
92	Tyler Stockton	DL	6'1"	285	SR
93	Connor Little	LB	6'3"	225	SO
94	Jarron Jones	DE	6'5"	299	FR
96	Kona Schwenke	DE	6'4"	290	JR

2012 ALABAMA CRIMSON TIDE 102

CHECK OUT MORE GREAT RELEASES FROM
MEGALODON ENTERTAINMENT LLC

Follow the **New Orleans Saints** through their amazing **Super Bowl XLIV (44) Championship** season, and re-experience every game, relive every score, and savor every victory.

Travel with The Saints on their long, often trying 43 years on the road to success.

Compare the stats on every Saints Quarterback.

THE NEW ORLEANS SAINTS STORY
THE 43-YEAR ROAD TO THE SUPER BOWL XLIV CHAMPIONSHIP

Dan Fathow

Who has the most yards, wins, and completions? Archie Manning, Drew Brees, Bobby Hebert, or Aaron Brooks? Find out which Saints coach has the best record and the most games. Sean Payton, Jim Mora, or Bum Phillips? This book is the perfect companion for new and long-time Saints fans alike.

ISBN 978-0-9800605-7-7

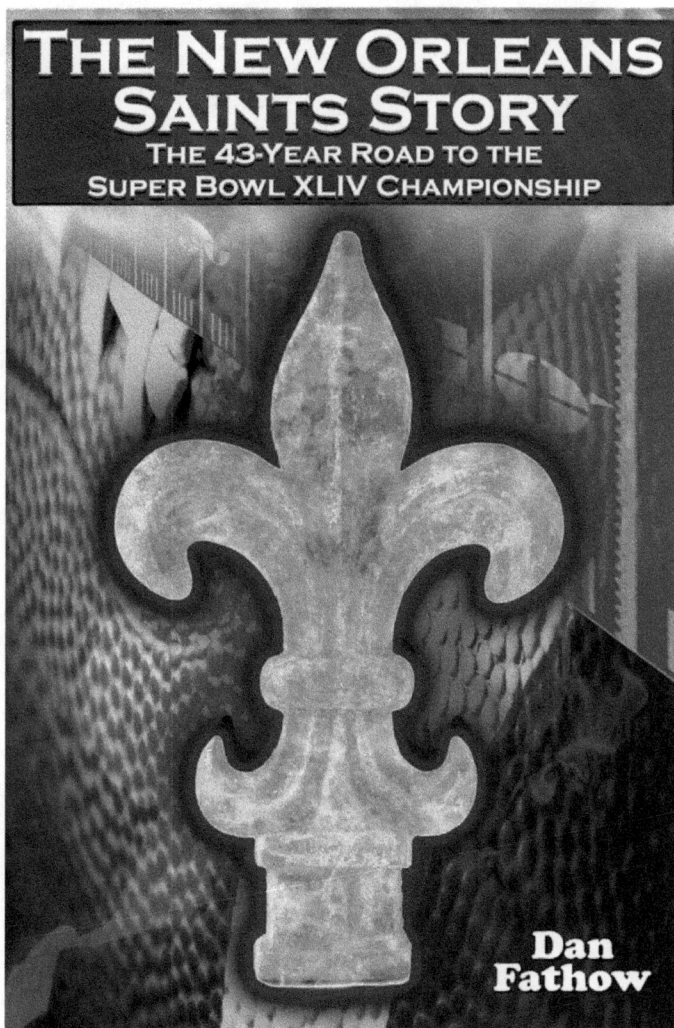

ALSO BY DAN FATHOW
STEINBRENNER: QUOTES, HITS, & LEGACY

Ever want to know what past-enemies Billy Martin, Yogi Berra, and Dave Winfield thought of their feuds with Steinbrenner? Want to know what Don Mattingly had to say following Steinbrenner's passing? Topics discussed range from Big Stein's suspension and subsequent lifetime ban from baseball; to his famous *Seinfeld* appearances, to Steinbrenner candidly commenting on his own flaws; to the appreciation of those he's helped over the years; to Steinbrenner's views on business, life philosophy, and charity; to criticisms of those he's scorned, to the numerous comments on his legacy from managers (Joe Torre, Lou Piniella, Joe Girardi), politicians (Bill Clinton, Rudy Giuliani), and current and former players (Derek Jeter, Wade Boggs, Darryl Strawberry, & many more). For an unbiased take on his life, Steinbrenner's stats as an owner are also crunched to give a factual perspective of his reign.

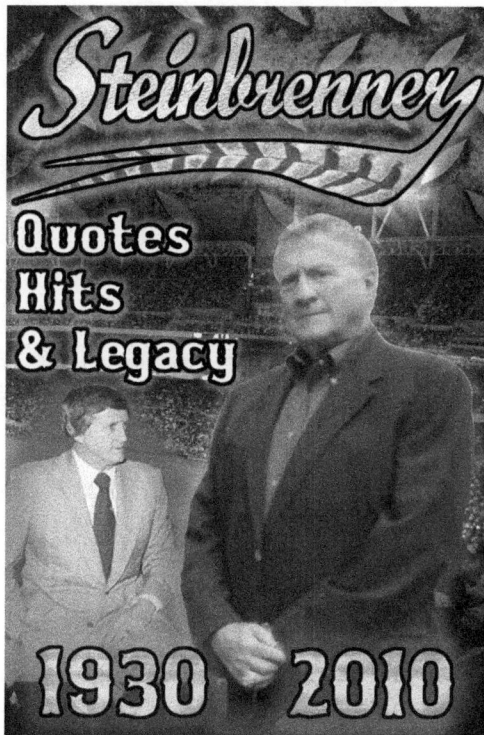

Steinbrenner's quotes cover such wide and interesting topics as Watergate, Pete Rose, Locker-Room Double Standards, Reggie Jackson, Alex Rodriguez, Yankee Tradition, Buying Championships, The Pine Tar Incident, General George S. Patton, His Alleged Fist-Fight with 2 Dodger Fans, and On How He'd Like to Be Remembered.

ISBN 978-0-9800605-7-7

www.ingramcontent.com/pod-product-compliance
Lightning Source LLC
Chambersburg PA
CBHW072205090426
42740CB00012B/2404